FINDING GOD'S WILL?

KEVIN T. BAUDER

Finding God's Will?

Copyright © 2021 Central Baptist Theological Seminary of Minneapolis

Published by:

Central Seminary Press

900 Forestview Ln N

Plymouth, MN 55441

(763) 417-8250

Printed by:

Nystrom Publishing Company, Inc.

9100 Cottonwood Lane North

Maple Grove, MN 55396

All Rights Reserved.

ISBN: 978-1-7363064-0-6

Library of Congress Control Number: 2021900153

Printed in the United States of America

❦ Created with Vellum

1
THE PROBLEM OF GOD'S WILL

Bill and John attended the same Bible college. Both were married. Both lived in the same housing complex. Both loaded trucks at a transit hub in a nearby city, and both their wives worked full time. Both felt pressed financially. Bill was particularly discouraged by his circumstances. He commented to John, "I'm beginning to think that Bible college isn't God's will for me."

John asked, "When you came here, were you convinced it was God's will?"

"Sure," said Bill. "If I hadn't thought so, I wouldn't have come."

"Then don't doubt in the darkness what you knew to be true in the light," said John. "You wouldn't want to miss God's will and have to settle for second best."

"I'm not sure that's how God's will works," answered Bill.

This discussion between Bill and John illustrates a couple of truths. The first is that Christians do not agree about "how God's will works." In fact, Christians do not even agree that God has an individual will that He wants each believer to follow. Second, those who think that God does have an individual will don't always agree about how they should discover it or how it should guide their lives. Entire volumes of rather technical theology—and even more volumes of nonsense—have been written about these questions.

Sometimes Christians get quite confused while trying to discern the will of God. Some find themselves paralyzed by their search for a will of God that seems to elude them. They are so afraid of making a wrong decision and ending up outside God's will that they can't seem to make any decision at all. They fritter away weeks, months, and even years while they flounder in their uncertainty. Ironically, they would probably do more of God's will if they were less concerned about discovering what it was.

Others confuse God's will with some purely subjective sense or feeling. They make their choices because they "feel led" or "have peace" about it. This approach has led to a variety of unfortunate results. Sometimes it produces arrogance, as with the young man who announces to a young woman that God's will is for her to marry him. Sometimes it leads to folly, as with the husband and father who abandons a good calling and uproots his family so that he can experiment with some new job or lifestyle for which he is ill-prepared and unsuited. Sometimes this approach to God's will even leads people into sin, like a woman I knew who felt that God's will was for her to divorce her husband and marry a different man. She couldn't understand why I didn't accept that choice as God's will for her life. For people like these, finding God's will doesn't really seem all that different from "going with your gut" or "following your heart."

Some Christians have reacted against these extremes by concluding that God has no particular will for His individual children, or, if He does, He keeps it hidden. They suggest that God's Word, the Bible, reveals sufficient wisdom for all of life's choices. As long as our choices do not contradict biblical precepts or principles, then they are within God's will. This approach has the advantage of eliminating a good bit of goofiness. As we shall see, God really does expect His children to employ wisdom in their choices. Several books of the Bible are called "wisdom literature" because they help us to understand how to make wise choices. Still, the wisdom-plus-nothing approach offers little help or hope to Christians who are struggling with truly difficult choices, especially when they acknowledge that those choices go beyond their limited wisdom. Believers have even despaired during dark hours because they believed that God was not willing to offer them guidance in making the most excruciating choices.

Is there a way to solve this problem? Can we avoid despair on the one hand but arrogance and paralysis on the other? Any solution will have to do two things. First, it will have to permit believers to seek genuine divine guidance for their decisions. Second, it will have to avoid treating this guidance as if it amounts to new revelation. I believe that such a middle way can be found—a way that honors the finality and sufficiency of

Scripture while providing believers with help for choices that the Bible does not directly address.

I haven't written this little book for people who want to argue about God's will (or whether He has one). I've written it for people who are hoping that God can and will guide them when they have to make perplexing choices. If you are one of those people, then I want to encourage you so that you can feel confident of God's guidance and blessing as you make decisions.

QUESTIONS FOR THOUGHT AND DISCUSSION

- What are some ways you have heard people talk about God's will? Which are biblical? Which are not?
- How have you tried to discern God's leading in your life?
- Have you ever faced a decision in which you felt that you had no idea what God's will might be? How did you finally make that decision?

2

GOD'S PROVIDENTIAL WILL

Does God have an individual will for each believer? Suppose He does not. If that is the case, then we must either deny the infinity of His wisdom and knowledge (because God doesn't know what is best for us) or else question His love and personal interest (because He doesn't care what is best for us). Yet God certainly does know what is best for each of His people. He certainly does wish the best for each of us. If God wishes the best for each believer while simultaneously knowing what is best—well, that is exactly to say that He has an individual will for each believer.

At some level, nearly all Christians acknowledge that God has a will for each individual Christian. Some have suggested, however, that God's will is always hidden or secret. Before we can evaluate that claim, we first have to ask, "What is God's hidden or secret will?" Here is where I have to ask you to do some fairly difficult thinking.

The notion that God has a hidden or secret will is tied to the doctrine of Providence, which states that God is actively working in and through His created order. Sometimes God has worked miraculously, but Providence is different from miracle. When God works miraculously, He works on nature from outside. Miraculous events have no natural explanations. When He works providentially, however, God works from inside nature. In other words, the doctrine of Providence requires double causation: every providential event has a natural cause, but it also has a divine cause.

Perhaps an example will help. Imagine some Christians who are living in a drought-stricken country. They begin to pray that God will send rain. Within days the sky clouds over and a thunderstorm drenches the parched fields. These believers give thanks to God for the rain, which they see as a blessing from His hand. At the same time, a meteorologist claims that the rain is the result of a cold front that has been approaching for a week—even before the believers began to pray. Who is right? The meteorologist, who sees a natural cause for the storm, or the Christians, who see the storm as a divine answer to their prayers?

The doctrine of Providence says that both answers are correct, as long as neither excludes the other. The thunderstorm is a genuinely natural event, but it is also a divine answer to prayer. God worked through the chain of meteorological causes to respond to His children's pleas.

According to the doctrine of Providence, this kind of double causation works both with natural events and with human events. Behind every human action is a double intention. One is the intention of the person who acts. The other is the intention of God. On the one hand, people genuinely and freely make their own choices and act out of their own intentions. Sometimes their intentions are evil. On the other hand, behind these human choices is also a divine intention. God permits the evil acts of sinful human beings because He intends to use them to advance His plan and to bring good to His people.

Joseph the patriarch provides an especially clear example of double intention. Joseph was sold into slavery by his brothers. That was an evil choice and an evil deed. The brothers intended harm to Joseph. Decades later Joseph was in power and his brothers were terrified that he would try to get even. Joseph reassured them, saying, "You meant evil against me, but God meant it for good" (Gen 50:20). The word *meant* (Hebrew *chashav*) is the same on both sides. Joseph's brothers had their intentions, which were bad—and Joseph never minimized their evil intentions. Nevertheless, Joseph recognized that God permitted their evil deed because He had His own intention, and God's intention was good. In the example of Joseph we can see that even the evil deeds of sinful humans are under the providential control of God.

God knows not only every event that occurs but also every event that will occur. Sometimes He causes those events directly. Other times He causes them indirectly by permitting bad things to happen. If He wished, He could prevent those bad events. Consequently, whatever happens is within His providential will. At some level we can say, "This is God's will for me," even when we are facing persecution or dreadful calamity. We are never outside of God's providential will. We cannot be.

Providence, however, is hidden. We usually don't see God's intentions as quickly or as clearly as we see the events themselves. Under normal circumstances, we can't perceive how those events—especially the calamitous ones—fit into God's plan. That is why theologians often refer to God's providential will as His *hidden* or *secret* will. Sometimes they also call it His *permissive* will, because He chooses to permit evil that He does not directly cause.

God's providential will encompasses every event in the life of every believer. Everything that happens to us always occurs within God's will, arranged by Him before the foundation of the world. These events always work together for good for those who love God, i.e., those who are called according to His purpose (Rom 8:28). Because it is secret, however, this providential will of God cannot be known in advance. It is found only in events as they occur, and it may not be understood until we are actually living in the presence of God.

Still, we ought to rejoice that God has a providential will for us. He arranges the events of our lives—even the unpleasant ones—so that they work together for good. The problem is that this secret will is exactly that: it is secret. It is not something that God tells us in advance. It gives us no help at all in making difficult choices, except perhaps to assure us that God intends to use even our bad choices to produce good for us (and that, to be sure, is no bad thing to know). Nobody, however, can seek the secret will of God or use it for guidance.

QUESTIONS FOR THOUGHT AND DISCUSSION

- Can you think of other biblical examples in which a sinful human being—or even a sinning spirit being—intended evil, but God turned it into good?
- Have you personally ever experienced calamitous circumstances that God turned around and used for good?
- Why can't we use God's providential (secret, hidden, or permissive) will to find guidance in our decisions?

3

THREE FALSE METHODS, AND A TRUE ONE

Should individual believers try to seek God's will for their lives at all? Some prominent theologians argue that we should not. They sometimes charge that if we ask for specific direction from God, then we are really asking for additional revelation beyond Scripture. To seek additional revelation, they insist, would be to deny the sufficiency of Scripture. Instead, they argue that the Bible provides all the principles that we need to make wise choices under every circumstance. Consequently, they claim that we do not need to know God's will specifically. Instead, we must simply exercise wisdom in our choices. For these people, any choice that we make using biblical wisdom is within God's will.

This position has much to commend it. The people who hold this view have produced some very good materials about how to make wise choices, and I have benefitted greatly from them. I think that what they teach about wisdom should be implemented by every believer when making choices. Too often (as I have already said) "knowing God's will" is simply the Christian equivalent of "going with your gut" or "following your heart," both of which are very bad ways of choosing.

A major movie producer and a leading manufacturer of greeting cards have built commercial empires by encouraging people to "follow your heart." That makes a catchy slogan, but what does it mean? Some people take this slogan to imply that our strongest emotional spasms ought to govern our choices. Furthermore, if we try to analyze or evaluate those powerful emotions, then we will delude ourselves into accepting something other than what is right for us. Other people use this slogan as an excuse to pour resources into some wished-for and desirable but fanciful future. Whatever the slogan means, however, it completely overlooks the fact that our hearts are immeasurably deceitful and desperately wicked (Jer 17:9). In fact, God's people are supposed to guard their hearts (Prov 4:3).

Yet "following your heart" is exactly what some Christians seem to mean when they talk about knowing God's will—with one slight difference. What is it? They assume that whatever they're feeling must be the voice of God to them. As they see it, following their heart is how they follow God. They further assume that by following their feelings, they will encounter only minor and temporary obstacles, to be followed by swift resolution leading to a cozy life.

Of course, life rarely works out in such a simple way, even for the most obedient believers. Unfortunately, many Christians who try to "follow their hearts" do very foolish things. Some of them end up feeling like God has let them down and failed to live up to His end of the bargain.

Faced with such spiritual disasters, the easiest response is to claim that God does not have a specific will for individual Christians. He simply wants every believer to employ biblical wisdom for every choice. That response does eliminate some very bad ways of making decisions, but it also carries a cost.

What is the cost? Just this: when the stakes are very high and all choices seem bad, we yearn to ask God to help us find a way forward. We recognize the fragility of our own wisdom, even if it is informed by the Scriptures. We long for some level of divine guidance and direction. This longing is no less genuine if we recognize that the Bible has a back cover and that God is no longer granting new revelations. The question is whether God could somehow help us, could provide some form of guidance, without endangering the finality and sufficiency of Scripture.

I believe the answer to that question is *yes*. If God knows and desires what is best for each believer, then He will not turn a deaf ear when His people cry out to Him for help. He has provided a way in which each of His children can face choices with confidence that their Father will direct their paths (Prov 3:5–6).

Nevertheless, Christians must beware of seeking God's will in the wrong ways and in wrong places. Three of these are particularly common. I intend to respond to these false ways of looking for God's will.

One is to seek God's will through signs and "fleeces." The word *fleece* comes from an episode in which the Old Testament judge Gideon sought to gain assurance of God's will by setting out a fleece (a sheep's skin). If God sent dew on the fleece but left the ground dry, or if God sent dew on the ground but left the fleece dry, then Gideon would know that God was directing (Jud 6:36–40). We say that people are "setting out a fleece" when they challenge God to reveal His will through some uncommon event or through some apparently chance occurrence such as the flip of a coin or the casting of a lot.

I was once a member of a church that was without a pastor. One of its missionaries was home from the field on furlough, and the church asked him to serve as interim pastor. By the end of three months, the missionary had decided that he would like to become the pastor of the church permanently. Unfortunately for him, the church's pulpit committee did not agree. The following Sunday the missionary stood in the pulpit and asked the church to cast lots to determine whether he or the pulpit committee was right. To its credit, the church refused to put God to this test.

God did use some of these ways of revealing His will in the past (Heb 1:1). Nothing in the Bible, however, indicates that He still intends for us to use these methods. Instead, the Bible teaches that God has now spoken to us in His Son, Jesus Christ (Heb 1:2). We have access to the teachings of Jesus only in the Bible. For us now to look for signs, to set out fleeces, or to cast lots is to neglect the Bible as God's final revelation to us. It is really to engage in superstition. Such activities are never the right way for us to find God's leading.

Another false method of discerning God's will is by

expecting Him to speak directly to us, whether through an audible voice, a dream or vision, or even an inner voice. To expect those experiences is exactly to seek additional revelation, which we must never do. Nobody today has a right to claim, "God told me," unless she or he can point to a verse of Scripture that is addressed to Church saints. Besides, this method has proven in practice to be a conspicuously bad way of determining God's leading. People who thought that they were surprised by the voice of God have often made disastrous decisions. The reason is simple: even if they do hear a voice, that voice is not God's.

A third false method for discovering God's will is called *bibliomancy*. That's a big word for a rather common practice. It involves opening the Bible, reading a verse (perhaps at random), and expecting that verse to reveal the will of God in answer to our question.

One day a preacher I was listening to commented that he had been trying to decide whether he should make a move to a new ministry. He told his people that he had been reading his Bible when he came to Acts 22:16, which begins with the words, "And now why tarriest thou?" He said that he knew God was speaking to him through these words, and that God's will was for him to move rather than "tarrying" or waiting. That is bibliomancy.

This method is grounded in the belief that God speaks through Scripture—and that belief is true, as far as it goes. Scripture is God's Word, inspired and inerrant. The problem is that the meaning and relevance of any verse must be determined by that verse's context. Every part of the Bible gains its significance from its place within the overall argument of the whole. To tear a text out of the whole, and to seek answers to questions that are foreign to the biblical context, is worse than superstition. It is an occult practice, not different in kind from seeking God's will by reading horoscopes, tea leaves, or sheep entrails.

So how should Christians seek to discern God's will for their lives? The answer to that question has several components. I will try to explain those in the coming chapters. For the moment, however, one point is worth emphasizing.

It is this: God's will always accords with Scripture rightly understood. Whatever other tools or techniques one uses to discern God's direction, the Bible always has the final word. God will never lead contrary to His revealed will in the Bible.

Of course, the Bible contains different expressions of God's will for different individuals at different times and in different places. God's will for Old Testament Israel (for example) is not identical with God's will for people in the Church. The two will share points of similarity and even identity, but they will also exhibit sharp contrasts. Knowing God's revealed will requires careful reading of the Bible and skillful interpretation.

Nevertheless, certain aspects of God's will are pretty clear. God's will is never for a believer to rob a gas station, murder an enemy, or abandon a spouse. God's will never includes envy, greed, bitterness, deceit, pride, or malice. God never wills His children to neglect their duties. God's will always entails holiness, justice, faith, hope, and love. Nobody whose conduct contradicts the teaching of Scripture can ever plead that she or he is doing God's will.

I believe that God has a specific will for each believer. Further, I believe that God is willing to provide direction or guidance to His children who seek it. On the other hand, I deny that following God's leading is a matter of additional revelation. I also deny that it is complicated or mysterious. The following chapters will outline how you or any believer can discern God's leading.

QUESTIONS FOR THOUGHT AND DISCUSSION

- Why would people seek God's will through signs, tests, and "fleeces"? Why would they engage in bibliomancy?
- Have you ever heard people claim that God was leading them to do something that you knew to be against Scripture? Why did they think that God was leading them?
- Have you ever had a sense that God was speaking directly to you, even though you did not hear an audible voice? What could create that impression, and how much weight should you give it in making your decisions?

4

START WITH WHAT YOU KNOW

If God is not granting further revelation beyond Scripture, then how can believers know His will for their lives? Specifically, how can they receive direction for their decisions without asking for additional revelation and consequently sacrificing the finality and sufficiency of Scripture? I have already commented that several components are involved in this process. I have also articulated the first component: God's will always accords with Scripture rightly understood. God never leads any of His children contrary to what the Bible teaches.

The second element in discerning God's will is closely related. It is simply that believers who want to *know* God's will must be prepared to *do* God's will. In other words, submission precedes knowledge.

This principle shouldn't surprise anyone. It follows the pattern established in the book of Proverbs. In that book of wisdom, the fear of the Lord is the beginning of knowledge (Prov 1:7). God refuses to answer those who call upon Him without first seeking Him; the fact that they do not fear the Lord shows that they really hate knowledge (1:28–29). A person who understands the fear of the Lord is the one who finds knowledge (2:5). This fear of the Lord involves hating pride, arrogance, and the evil way (8:13). It is the beginning of wisdom (9:10), and the knowledge of the Holy One is understanding. The fear of the Lord gives His people strong confidence and is a fountain of life (14:26–27). This fear precedes instruction in wisdom, just as humility precedes true honor (15:33). It leads people to depart from evil (16:6). It tends toward life, results in settled satisfaction, and spares one from calamity (19:23).

These and similar verses imply that God's will is not something that we can know in the abstract. We do not have the privilege of placing God's will under scrutiny or of sitting in judgment over it. We are not permitted to find out what God's direction is so that we can then decide whether we will follow it. If we are not genuinely interested in doing God's will, then God has no reason to help us discover His will. God directs those who are willing to obey.

These observations lead to a question: Who *is* willing to obey? Are we? It is easy to say that we are willing, but sometimes it is much harder actually to do what God says. Jesus once told a parable about a father who told his two sons to go work in the vineyard (Matt 21:28–32). The first son refused and said that he would not. This son, however, later changed his mind and went to work. The second son said that he would go to the vineyard, but he never did. The point of the parable is that not everyone who professes to be willing really is. It also implies that not everyone who initially resists obedience is ultimately unwilling.

Jesus taught something similar in John 7. This episode occurred when He was in the temple teaching. The Jewish leadership raised questions about the legitimacy of what Jesus taught. Jesus replied that His teaching was from God (7:16). Nevertheless, the divine origin of His teaching would only be recognized by those who wanted to do God's will (7:17). Jesus then pointed out that His critics had received God's law from Moses, but they did not obey it (7:19). Jesus was saying that their unwillingness to obey God disqualified them from recognizing the divine origin of His teaching. Only those who are willing to obey God can know His will.

If that is so, then how do we judge whether we ourselves are really willing to obey God's will? The answer is obvious from the foregoing passages. The person who is willing is not the one who *professes to obey*, but the one who *actually obeys*. Our willingness to do God's will becomes evident only when we actually do it. We are willing to do God's will if and only if we are presently obeying God's will.

How can we obey God's will before He makes it known? The answer to this question is painfully simple. God has already disclosed His will, or most of it, in a clear and objective manner. The text of Scripture is written to make God's will known. At minimum, the teachings of the epistles apply directly to Church saints. While we may niggle at some points of interpretation and application, God has surely made His will in general clear enough for any believer to follow.

Of course, the Bible does not give us direct, personal guidance for every possible decision. Still, we cannot claim that we want God's leading in our unique circumstances if we are presently disobeying His revealed will in Scripture. That kind of conduct shows that we are merely pretending. If we know that we are disobeying God's revealed will while we are pretending to agonize over His individual leading, then we are guilty of flat hypocrisy.

Believe me, professing Christians play this game. When I was a pastor I once had a woman come to my study to ask whether God could lead her to marry a divorced man. I told her that Christians take different views of divorce and remarriage, and I tried to give her the categories for making a wise and biblical choice. She was quite upset with even the most relaxed understanding of the biblical text; she saw it as impossibly narrow. Later I learned that she was already sleeping with someone else's husband. She was actively trying to destroy his marriage so that she could capture the man for herself. She never had any interest in doing God's will, even though she initially pretended to.

Granted, that is an extreme example, but it clarifies the point. God is only interested in leading those who want to do His will. We demonstrate our intention to do God's will by obeying the part of His will that we already know. The part that we know is revealed in the text of Scripture. If we refuse to obey what we know the Bible teaches, then all our talk about doing God's will rings false.

On the other hand, habitual obedience will clear up an amazing number of perplexities in our lives. If we are committed to doing God's will, and if we are actually obeying that part of His will that we already know (because it is revealed in Scripture), then we do not have to worry about what we ought to do under most circumstances. We can simply entrust our paths to the God who providentially oversees our lives. We do not need to agonize in prayer, for instance, before deciding whether to eat Kellogg's Corn Flakes or Post Toasties for breakfast.

The principle here is quite simple. If you want to know God's will, then you must begin by doing God's will. Your obedience to what you already know is the outward exhibition of a heart that genuinely wishes to follow God's leading.

QUESTIONS FOR THOUGHT AND DISCUSSION

- Do you really want to do God's will?
- Are you presently trying to do all of God's will that you know? Or have you been neglecting or disobeying some aspect of what you know God wants you to do?
- How would you counsel a person who claimed to be seeking God's will in one area while fighting it in another?

5
KNOW YOUR DUTIES

John Buck is a junior-level manager for a national corporation where he has been advancing through the ranks. One day his boss stops by to offer John a new position as manager of a plant in a distant part of the country. The job comes with a pay increase of $15,000 per year. John has one week to give his boss an answer.

Both John and his wife Anne believe that he is ready to take on the responsibility. If he rejects the promotion, then he might not be given another chance. They are concerned, however, about their three teenage children, all of whom would be pulled out of their schools in the middle of the year. Their concerns increase when, after investigating the city where they would be living, they cannot find a rightly-ordered New Testament church with a pastor who actually preaches the Bible.

Their present church is small, but its members are committed to the Lord. Its pastor expounds the Scriptures accurately, applies them well, and is deeply interested in the lives of the congregation's members. John has served this church as a deacon for ten years. Anne is the church's only accompanist. Many of the other members are retirees. They support the church, but the Bucks' giving makes a substantial difference.

John and Anne believe that God has a specific direction for them in this choice. They genuinely want to follow the Lord's leading. They are already trying to obey as much of the Bible's teaching as they understand. What considerations will help them to determine how God might direct in their present circumstances?

One question they might ask is this: "What are my duties?" Every duty is an obligation, a responsibility that people owe to themselves or others. All people have duties. They owe responsibilities to God, nation, family, church, and calling. Some duties are intrinsic and inescapable. Others are freely assumed but binding once accepted. For example, vows are not normally obligatory, but once sworn become compulsory (Num 30).

What duties do the Bucks owe? How should those duties affect John's choice about the new job?

Clearly John and Anne owe a duty to their three teenage children. As parents they are responsible to rear their children in the nurture and admonition of the Lord (Eph 6:4). While the text of Scripture does not specify every method by which that is done, John and Anne can easily foresee the disruption that will follow if they pull their children away from their school, church, and established home in the middle of the school year.

Furthermore, the responsibility to make disciples does not belong to parents alone (Matt 28:19–20).

Making disciples is the business of local churches, and without a good church discipleship almost always suffers. For New Testament Christians, church membership is not optional. It is obligatory. If John and Anne cannot find (or plant) a good church, then they and their children will lose an important center of spiritual nourishment, encouragement, warning, instruction, shared labor, and corporate worship. This deficiency will certainly affect the entire family. Just as importantly, by voluntarily placing themselves in a situation where they know that they cannot find a good church, they will be disobeying God.

The Bucks also owe something to their present congregation. Joining a church is not like joining a club. One becomes a member of a New Testament church by entering into a covenant. A covenant is an oath or vow that the members swear to one another. It affirms their intention together to be a church, and it also defines what their responsibilities as members will look like. While a church covenant is not a lifelong obligation, it is not a casual obligation and it should not be easily abandoned. If John and Anne move away, they will leave a void that cannot be easily filled.

On the other hand, John does not have a duty to make more money or to advance in the company. Granted, he does owe some level of loyalty and cooperation to his employers. Still, unless he is bound in some way (such as a contract), this obligation is lesser and more relative than the others.

Of course, it is possible for a duty to an employer to become completely inflexible. One example is when the National Guard deploys its soldiers. A Christian guardsman is duty-bound to go where his (or her) unit is sent. Those circumstances eliminate the dilemma because they eliminate the choice. They also raise the question of what duties might prevent someone from making that kind of inflexible commitment in the first place.

Sometimes circumstances simply do away with all choices. When that happens, believers can be sure that God is providentially directing their lives, even if the circumstances are terrible. Now they need no longer seek God's direction. Instead, they must seek ways to glorify Him under the circumstances into which He has directed them. They must do the best they can with a bad situation for as long as they have to, but when they are once again free to choose for themselves they should make the choice that enables them to fulfill the greatest number of duties in the best way possible.

Occasionally the difficult circumstances may be the result of previous bad choices. For example, a seminarian who goes into debt will be less free to follow the Lord's leading into a small pastorate or onto the mission field. The seminarian has become a borrower, and borrowers are enslaved to lenders (Prov. 22:7). A person who owes money will be working for the creditor until the debt is paid. God's will for indebted people is to repay their creditors as honorably as possible. Until that step has been taken, debtors lack freedom to choose. Their duty is to pay what they owe.

Any effort to discern God's leading for particular choices should begin with the question, "What are my duties?" Each of us owes multiple duties, and God will never lead us to neglect any of them. We cannot rightly plead God's will as an excuse to escape from the obligations that we owe.

Everyone has duties. Finding God's direction must begin by acknowledging these duties and seeking to fulfill them. Christians who develop a keen sense of duty and a determination to fulfill all duties often find that many seemingly-difficult choices simply vanish. Discovering God's leading will become a much simpler process.

QUESTIONS FOR THOUGHT AND DISCUSSION

- What duties do you owe to your parents? Your spouse? Your children? Your extended family? Your church? Your employer? Your country?
- Can you think of other duties that you might have? Have you made promises that you must keep? Have you agreed to other obligations that you must fulfill?
- Do these duties place any decisions out of bounds for you? If so, what are some decisions that you must not even consider?

6
PRAY ABOUT IT

Throughout this discussion I have assumed that God has an individual will for each Christian and that His direction can be discerned. To this point, I have described criteria for determining God's will that are straightforward and objective. God's leading never contradicts Scripture rightly understood. The person who wishes to know God's will must be willing to do God's will, and this willingness is characterized by actual obedience to as much of God's will as is already known. God's will is always for Christians to fulfill their duties.

The remaining criteria are less straightforward. They are more subjective, though they can be quite as important as the objective criteria. Employing these criteria requires wisdom and a sense of balance. Consequently, those who wish to seek God's leading need to fulfill at least one prerequisite.

That prerequisite is prayer. To receive wisdom from God we have to ask for it. If we ask, however, we will receive it generously (Jas 1:5). Since wisdom is necessary to discern God's will, the process of seeking God's direction must be bathed in prayer.

You may wonder why I have waited until this point to mention prayer. If it is so important, then shouldn't it take priority over all other considerations? Shouldn't I have discussed it first?

In reply, I ask you to remember that the first considerations are objective. We know them because God has spoken. First, God reveals a good bit of His will in the Bible. God's leading never contradicts what God has revealed. Second, when we seek God's will, we must begin by obeying His revealed will. Third, even our duties are plain because they are revealed in Scripture.

In other words, we do not have to ask God what His will is in any of those matters. His will is already settled, stated for us in black and white. We determine God's revealed will, not by praying for divine guidance, but by reading the Bible. We do not have to ask God whether His will for us is to embezzle from our employer. We do not have to pray about the decision to abandon a spouse. We needn't plead for guidance about using methamphetamine recreationally. We should find no ambiguity over questions like whether we should covenant with a local church, testify of God's grace, or give money toward God's work. In all of these matters, God has already told us what His will is.

When we pray about matters that God has already told us, we might as well admit that we have not been paying attention to Him. If we had paid attention, we would already have our answers. These are not matters that require discernment. We don't need any special, spiritual insight to decide whether to view pornography or to engage in a drunken weekend bender. When it comes to things like these, we don't need to pray about God's will. What we need to do is to obey God's will as we already know it. If we pray about such activities, we reduce piety to a game and Christianity to a show. In effect, we are mocking God—and God refuses to be mocked (Gal 6:7).

The time to pray for God's direction is when Scripture by itself does not give us clear guidance. That is when we must come to our Father and humbly ask Him for wisdom that we do not possess in ourselves. It is the time to ask Him to make clear to us the best way forward.

Of course, we do not typically pray specifically for the small, everyday choices. We do not pause at the medicine cabinet to seek divine guidance concerning Crest versus Colgate. We do not prayerfully ponder whether we ought to eat the green beans or the Brussels sprouts. Instead, we ask God to direct our paths, and we prayerfully commit the keeping of our ways to Him. As the normal decisions of life come our way, we roll along with them and simply make the choice that seems best at the moment, trusting God to oversee our determinations.

Sometimes, however, we are confronted with choices that stop us with serious consequences. We do not make these decisions automatically, because we fear making a bad choice. We want to make the best choice possible, but it may not be obvious to us. Those are the times when we need the wisdom that is from above (Jas

3:17). Those are the times when we absolutely must seek God's guidance.

When we are perplexed we may spend days or even weeks in prayer over a serious decision. If it is a decision that affects our families, then we should ask our spouses and perhaps other family members to pray with us. We might solicit the prayers of our Christian brothers and sisters. Sometimes we will even commit ourselves to fasting so as to give ourselves more fully to prayer. The prayer of a righteous person has great power (Jas 5:16).

Nevertheless, prayer is not a magic formula to secure a personal revelation. We should not expect the answer to be written in the sky or to become audible to the ears of the soul. We should expect no signs and we should trust no sudden, overwhelming convictions. Such things are too easily counterfeited—and powers other than God know how to produce them. The prayer for guidance will be answered through the exercise of wisdom, judgment, and discretion.

That is where the subjective criteria come in. Exercising wisdom requires us to appeal to several sources and to weigh several considerations. What these sources include will be the subject of the following chapters.

QUESTIONS FOR THOUGHT AND DISCUSSION

- Should we pray about every single decision that we make, such as which brand of toothpaste to use or which cereal to eat for

breakfast? Why or why not? If so, how should we pray?
- What kind of decisions do you regularly pray about? Why do you pray about these and not others?
- If you were facing a major decision, do you have people who you would ask to pray with you? Would these people be different, depending on the nature of the decision?

7
INFORM YOURSELF

A few months ago I received a phone call from a colleague, a former student who went on to serve in pastoral ministry for a decade. He told me that he was trying to decide whether to remain in his current pastorate or whether to go back to school. He thought that he might like to teach in a Bible college or seminary someday, which would require a doctor's degree. He asked for my counsel as he weighed his choices.

His request reflected a number of important considerations in seeking God's will. First, he was choosing deliberately, refusing to allow momentary emotions to determine his direction. Second, he was seeking counsel—a matter I'll have more to say about in a later chapter. Third, and perhaps most importantly, he was looking for information. He wanted to know what he could expect if he were to pursue an academic doctorate, and he wanted to know about teaching opportunities once he had the degree.

I'm afraid that my reply wasn't overly encouraging. I explained that few people can anticipate the kind of labor and sacrifice that goes into earning a Ph.D. or Th.D. Fewer still understand that the pressures must be borne by both the students and their families. Yet this price must be paid: an earned doctorate is the union card for teaching in higher education. I said all of this because I wanted my friend to know about the demands that he would face if he left his pastorate for further education.

That wasn't the end of the bad news. Doctors of Philosophy now saturate the academy. Even large universities are shifting toward using adjunct rather than full-time teachers. Within conservative Christianity this situation is worsened by the fact that many of our schools have closed over the past decade or two, and most of those that remain are only half the size they once were. Every man who leaves the pastorate for doctoral study needs to think seriously about what he will do for a living once he has earned the degree. He could go back into the pastorate, of course, but nobody needs a Ph.D. to be a good pastor.

What was the right decision for my colleague? I really didn't know. In any event, he didn't want to know what *my* will might be, but what *God's* leading was. For discerning God's leading, he was doing the right thing by gaining as much information as he could.

The Bible is full of both examples and principles that merge God's will with adequately-informed judgment. God's will was for Joshua to conquer the land, but Joshua still sent investigators to gather information from Jericho (Josh 2). Those who hope to pass wise judgments are obligated to gain information from multiple witnesses (Deut 19:15; 2 Cor 13:1). Acting without knowledge is not good (Prov 19:2). A person who makes a pronouncement without listening to the facts is a fool (Prov 18:13).

Ignorance is never a virtue in finding God's direction. To be sure, circumstances sometimes force us to make decisions about which we are poorly informed. Furthermore, we almost always wish that we had more information than we do. We can never become omniscient, and some little thing that we don't know might be the one thing that would have changed our minds. Granted, we cannot learn everything—but that is no excuse for not learning all we can.

Informing yourself and seeking God's will are not mutually exclusive activities. God does not usually lead in a vacuum. He uses several factors to create in us an impression of what His direction might be. The more attention we pay to these factors, the more likely we are to understand what God wishes us to do. One of the most important factors is information. By learning all that we can about our decision, we are giving God something to work with as He leads.

Consider a man who is offered a promotion that will require him to move his family to a distant city. He ought to know exactly what his new responsibilities will entail and who he will be working with. He ought to learn all he can about the city, both in terms of its opportunities and in terms of its problems. He ought to search in advance for churches in that city, and, if possible, he ought to visit some of them and talk to their pastors.

He should also inform himself about the subjective responses of the people who will be affected by his decision. How will his new co-workers perceive him? How does his wife feel about the move? How do his children feel about it? On the other hand, how will his employers respond if he declines? These matters may be outside his control, but he still needs to take them into account. How people feel is part of the information that should go into his decision.

Every kind of decision requires different information. No single rule can specify exactly what sort of information you must gather for any given choice. The only rule is to gain as much relevant information as possible before the choice has to be made. Informing yourself is necessary if you intend to exercise due diligence when making decisions.

I have heard Christian leaders dismiss the exercise of due diligence by denouncing it as "human wisdom." They are half right. It *is* wisdom—but it is not merely human. It is the care that God expects His people to exercise before committing themselves to a course of action. Even Jesus thought that a man who was going to build a tower should not begin construction until he knew how much the project would cost (Luke 14:28). Too many Christian leaders have wrecked ministries—and people's lives—because they did not bother to inform themselves before announcing some course of action and proclaiming it to be "God's will." Too many people have said, "I'm living by faith," when what they meant was "I'm following an impulse and doing it blindly."

Ignorance is not faith. Ignorance does not foster

faith. Ignorance is not a substitute for faith. Ignorance is never a virtue. Instead, information is a tool that the faithful use whenever possible while seeking God's direction. David trusted God to deliver him from Saul, but he also trusted the information that Jonathan brought him (1 Sam 20).

God places us in positions in which we have to make choices. In those choices He certainly knows what direction is best for us, but He does not simply tell us what to do. Instead, He uses those decisions as opportunities to grow us in maturity and wisdom. Maturity and wisdom involve the capacity for sound judgment. For that reason, seeking God's leading usually requires the exercise of sound judgment. The simple truth is that informed judgments are usually sounder than uninformed ones.

Do you want God's will? If you are already yielded to Him, obeying Him, fulfilling your duties to the best of your ability, and praying about your choice, then the next thing you need to do is to inform yourself. The information you gain may be exactly the instrument that God uses to disclose His direction for your life.

QUESTIONS FOR THOUGHT AND DISCUSSION

- What sort of information might you need to make a choice about a career? About purchasing a home? About choosing a spouse? About choosing a church?
- What sort of information should a church have before deciding to relocate or build a

building? Before deciding to start a school? Before deciding to call a pastor?
- How could you legitimately gain the information that you need for the above choices?

8

SEEK GODLY COUNSEL

God knows exactly those choices that will bring the greatest good into your life. Perhaps those are not the choices that will result in the greatest *apparent* good, especially in the short run—I'll have more to say about that in a later chapter. But God knows who He wants you to be, and He knows which choices will bring you to that goal.

To deny that God is able to lead you in making those choices would be pointless. God promises that if we trust in the Lord and acknowledge Him, He will direct our paths (Prov 3:6). In the Bible, He often directed His people through special revelation. Sometimes He directed them in other ways. Of course, He still directs us through the revelation that is recorded in Scripture, but there is no particular reason to think that He cannot direct us in non-revelatory ways as well.

One of the ways in which God leads us to the right choices is through godly counsel. What Proverbs 11:14 says about nations is also true of individuals: without guidance we are in danger, but deliverance can be found in the abundance of counselors. Proverbs also teaches that where people fail to seek counsel their plans are often frustrated, but counsel from multiple sources helps them to make good plans (Prov 15:22). Good counsel results in workable plans (Prov 20:18). Relying upon many counselors results in safety (Prov 24:6). *Not* seeking counsel is the mark of a fool (Prov 12:15).

Clearly, God intends us to seek counsel. We may not need counsel for ordinary, mundane choices, such as whether we should wear the blue tie or the red one (though even here many men would do well to heed the counsel of their wives). When it comes to the big choices, however, we should not make a decision without gaining counsel.

If we want to get any help from counsel, we need to choose wise and careful counselors. Bad counsel can lead us seriously astray, as it did with Rehoboam (1 Ki 12:1–23). Confronted by the people of Israel with his sinful excesses, Rehoboam took the counsel of foolish young men rather than wise older ones. That counsel brought disaster into his life. We should not expect to receive good counsel from people who are only going to tell us what we want to hear. We should also beware of counselors who only tell us what *they* want us to hear.

I know of churches where the pastor tells the people never to make a major decision without asking him for counsel. When they go to the pastor for counsel, he first listens to them describe their possible choices. He then pronounces God's will for their lives. A very high percentage of the time, God's will turns out to be the decision that is best for the pastor's ministry or even for him personally.

In the face of such arrogance, we might easily grow cynical about pastoral counsel. That is an over-reaction; the principle itself is a sound one. If a pastor knows his people, his God, and his Bible, he ought to be in a position to offer sound counsel.

Pastoral counsel, however, rarely involves telling people what they ought to do. The only appropriate time for a pastor to tell people what is God's will for their lives is when a clear biblical requirement is at stake. Otherwise, a pastor's main responsibility is to help people think through the decisions that they must make. He should guide them through the various considerations (including biblical principles) that ought to inform their decision. He might point out any circumstances that could affect their choice. He will help them to understand any personal giftedness, abilities, and proclivities that might shape their decisions. In short, he will play a supporting role, assisting people to exercise wisely their prerogatives as believer-priests before the Lord.

What is true of pastoral counsel should be true of other counsel as well. Counsel does not usually consist in telling other people what to do. Only very immature people need or want to have decisions handed to them. Mature people should wish to make their own choices, and they should exercise sound judgment when they do. Offering counsel is a matter of helping them to be sure that they have weighed every necessary consideration before making their choice.

Earlier I cited a list of texts from the book of

Proverbs. These texts typically recommend getting counsel from a group or "multitude" of counselors. These counselors should normally be people with knowledge, expertise, or insight into the kind of decision you're making. They should be people who know you. They should also be people with experience, often older, who have done lots of living and have shown that they know how to make good decisions.

For married people, husbands or wives are often best equipped to offer good counsel. Our spouses know us like no one else does. They usually understand our choices in greater detail than any other. Here I can speak from experience: my wife is my wisest counselor. Her insights have spared me from trouble on many occasions. I would not dream of making a major decision without discussing it with her first. Furthermore, I would not make a decision that she was convinced was wrong. The process of making home-shaping decisions is and ought to be shared.

Perhaps some might worry that for a wife to share in making household decisions could violate marital submission (Eph 5:22–24, 33). It does not. Rather, for a husband to ensure that his wife has a voice in those decisions is one of the ways in which he implements the love that he owes to his wife (Eph 5:25–33). Even a very deferential wife needs to be involved in decisions that affect her future, and a loving husband will make sure that she is. A husband who fails to solicit his wife's counsel, or one who neglects or ignores it when it is offered, is simply a fool. Of course, the same could be said of wives who neglect their husbands' counsel.

Besides spouses, parents often make the best counselors. Even unbelieving mothers and fathers can sometimes offer surprising insight into the decisions that their grown children must make. Parents who know the Lord and the Bible are some of the best counselors in the world. In any event, seeking parental counsel is part of honoring one's father and mother (Eph 6:2–3). At more than sixty years of age, I still treasure my parents' counsel before making most major decisions. My mom and dad are wise people, and I want to take advantage of their insight as long as I can.

True friends also make wonderful counselors. A true friend is one who is willing to wound you when necessary (Prov 27:5). Like pastors, spouses, and parents, friends cannot counsel by making decisions for you. What they can do is to make sure you've examined every legitimate factor that ought to affect your decision. They can point out any considerations that you may have neglected. They can talk with you, pray for you, and help you to weigh the various elements that affect your decision.

On rare occasions we may be confronted with decisions that must be made in isolation. Under normal circumstances, however, we ought to surround ourselves with as many wise counselors as we can. We should talk to them freely, hear them fully, and weigh their counsel carefully. Our counselors cannot take responsibility for our decisions, but they can help us to find God's leading.

QUESTIONS FOR THOUGHT AND DISCUSSION

- Who are the first three people whom you might ask for counsel in your most important decisions? Why these three?
- Have you ever made a decision for which you did not seek counsel but later wished you had?
- Can you envision any important decision for which you might not seek counsel? Why not?

9

CONSIDER YOUR CIRCUMSTANCES

In previous chapters I have outlined several considerations that you should weigh when seeking to discern God's leading in your life. Obviously, you should avoid wrong ways of knowing God's will, such as inner voices, dreams, "fleeces," and misuse of Scripture. Instead, you should begin by obeying God's will as revealed in Scripture: your obedience is evidence of your commitment to know and do God's will. Then you should prioritize faithfulness to duties. You should bathe decisions in prayer. You should gather all the information you can that affects your decision. You should seek the counsel of people who know you and who know God.

Now I suggest another consideration that will help you to discover God's direction. It will probably seem pretty obvious, but it still bears stating. It is to pay attention to circumstances.

Before I go on, I ought to tell you that some Christians disagree with me. Their motivations are good:

they believe that walking by faith is opposed to walking by sight, and they wish to walk by faith. They also believe that taking account of circumstances is walking by sight. Therefore, to heed circumstances is a failure to walk by faith. Furthermore (these brothers and sisters remind us), whatever is not of faith is sin.

I actually agree with them!—but only to a point. When biblical commands or promises appear to contradict circumstances, then we owe loyalty to whatever God says. Abraham believed God, even when circumstances appeared to make the fulfillment of God's promises impossible (Heb 11:17–19). When our circumstances mean that taking God at His word will cost us everything, then we ought to obey God anyway.

If we are not careful, we can sometimes forget that the Christian life is a life of faith. God does lead us to make sacrifices for the furtherance of the gospel and the wellbeing of our fellow believers. The will of God is not always for us to do the thing that will result in the greatest personal profit and advancement. Consequently, when I suggest that we ought to pay attention to circumstances, I am not saying that we should always do the thing that most obviously advances our own interests.

We must walk by faith, but Christian faith cannot rightly be placed in anything except what God has said. If we know what God has said, however, then we do not have to ask about His will. We only have to do what He has told us. We only wonder how God is leading us when we don't know of any biblical revelation that would make our decision for us. On the other hand, if we do not have God's clearly spoken will, then we would be arrogant to act as if our decision rested upon the promises of divine revelation. To say it in different words, we have no right to assert our own will and then to act as if we had a promise from God. Our own impressions and decisions are not a proper object of faith. If we insist upon following our own will in spite of circumstances that render it unattainable, then we cannot claim to be exercising faith.

To cite an extreme (if somewhat silly) example, I may believe that God is leading me to offer my services as an accompanist in a church that lacks one. The problem is that I cannot play a musical instrument. For me to accompany a congregation would require not merely personal willingness but an outright miracle of the sort that God nowhere promises. My circumstances ought to tell me that God is not leading me to make such a decision. If I do volunteer to be an accompanist and persist in that decision, then my perseverance is not an act of faith but of arrogance.

Paying attention to circumstances is simply a matter of common sense. Paul was using common sense and paying attention to circumstances when he told the centurion not to sail from Fair Havens until spring (Acts 27:9–10). When things went wrong, Paul even reminded the centurion that he should have listened (Acts 27:21). Circumstances should indeed be taken into account when seeking God's leading. Simply heeding our circumstances can prevent some very bad decisions.

I've made some of those decisions myself. After I graduated from college, my wife and I moved to Denver so I could go to seminary. At Thanksgiving time we wanted to drive back to her parents' home in Iowa, then on to my parents' home in Wisconsin for their silver wedding anniversary. We left Denver in the middle of an early snowstorm. The authorities were asking people to stay off the roads, but I reasoned, "How bad could it be?"

It was worse than I could have imagined. Before we had gone fifty miles up Interstate 76 we found ourselves in the middle of a blizzard. The snow was so thick and the wind so severe that I couldn't see the hood of the car in front of the windshield. We stuck in drift after drift until we buried ourselves in one that we couldn't get free of. Fortunately, I was able to contact a snow plow on my CB radio. He was about to leave the highway himself, but first he picked us up and dropped us at a truck stop diner. That night we slept on the restaurant floor alongside several other stranded motorists.

I had been in Midwestern snowstorms, but never anything like that. I did not know how to judge the weather on the high plains. Because I failed to consider the circumstances, I made a choice that could have been deadly. On future trips, Colorado weather was always a consideration that I weighed when deciding whether to travel.

God expects us to exercise sound judgment. Sound judgment requires us to take account of circumstances. When we are seeking God's direction for decisions in our lives, our circumstances are among the factors that God expects us to consider.

Having said that, let me add that circumstances may not determine our choices. Many of our best decisions will lead us into difficult circumstances. For example, people who decide to become physicians will have to spend years in college, more years in medical school, and still more years in residency. These future doctors will have to pass many difficult examinations, endure many long shifts, and perhaps experience a level of poverty while trying to complete their preparation. If they can overcome these obstacles, however, they can find great satisfaction in reaching the goal. If someone can't even get into a medical school, however, God's will is probably not for that person to become a physician.

We need to weigh circumstances with a bit of skill and discernment. We need not take every opportunity that we are offered. We will walk past many open doors without going through them. By the same token, not every closed door is bolted shut. Some may open when we rattle the handle or turn the lock, and others may open later on. Sometimes circumstances may not make our decision for us, but we should always examine the circumstances and take them into account.

QUESTIONS FOR THOUGHT AND DISCUSSION

- What role do you think that "closed doors" and "open doors" should play in making decisions?
- Should you go through every open door? Is that even possible?
- What might God be saying when He closes a door?

10

ACCOUNT FOR YOUR INCLINATIONS

Some Christians think that ignoring circumstances is a mark of spirituality. The Bible, however, never rebukes us for taking circumstances into account. Only if we possess direct, divine revelation should we turn our backs upon circumstances.

Some Christians also denigrate another factor that helps us to find God's leading. When we are trying to discern the Lord's direction, we should also consider our inclinations. We should ask, "What would I really like to do?"

Too often, Christians assume that God's will is an ugly, repugnant thing that they would prefer to avoid if they could. Of course, sometimes God does lead us into difficult places. Left to themselves, Jeremiah would not have chosen to be thrown into the well and Daniel would not willingly have entered the lions' den. In those cases, however, obedience to God's revealed will was clearly at stake. When God directs us into unpleasant circumstances, He usually does it in ways that are unmistakable and even unavoidable.

God does not usually lead us in ways that thwart our inclinations. In fact, Jesus promised rest for our souls. He told us that His yoke is easy and His burden is light (Matt 11:30). David taught that when we delight in the Lord, He gives us the desires of our heart (Psalm 37:4). In other words, God typically leads us to want the things that He wants to give us. Normally, doing God's will is a joy, something that we can look forward to with cheerful anticipation.

How often do we hear the phrase, "I surrendered to the Lord's will"? This phrase makes it sound as if the only way that God can get us to knuckle under is to batter us until we lower our colors in defeat. While such things can happen, they are not the norm. Why should we suppose that God, who is capable of shaping our desires, would incline us not to want what He wants for us? The notion would be almost ridiculous, except for the fact that some Christians seem to assume that God works just that way.

On the contrary, God prepares us for what He wants us to do. He equips us for the things to which He calls us. If we are seeking Him and delighting in Him, He inclines us toward the things that He sees as our greatest good. We should expect to find ourselves wanting the kind of things that God wants for us.

Granted, sometimes we are afraid of situations simply because we've never experienced them and they seem intimidating. Facing challenges like that is part of maturing. It is also part of finding God's leading. Once we try the things that we fear, we often discover that they delight us—provided that we don't close ourselves off to that possibility. If we are willing to experience the unfamiliar, God will use those experiences to create new loves within us. He may then use those loves to lead us.

I live in greater Minneapolis, where people "go up north" for their vacations. Once when I was preaching in northern Minnesota I asked a man where his family went for vacation while everybody from Minneapolis was going up north to his town. He smiled and said, "The further north you go, the better it gets."

Not everybody loves the north, but some people do. They would feel like they were melting in Houston heat and humidity. God may well be preparing those people to serve him in International Falls, Calgary, or Fairbanks.

For nearly a decade I lived in Dallas, Texas. I thought it was funny when the temperature would drop below seventy and people would put on overcoats. I'm a Michigan boy, and for me sixty degrees is shirt-sleeve weather. I can still remember being told as a child, "No, you can't go swimming until it warms up to seventy." But those people who love the heat may be the very people God wants to use in places like Tampa or Mobile.

No lie of the devil has been more effective than the notion that God's will is some ugly, horrible thing that we would never really want to choose. But think about it: would a kind and gracious God really treat us that way? Would He make His will a punitive thing? Doesn't it make sense that He would create in us the desire to do the kind of thing He wants us to do?

At the time I married I had no sense of vocation, no idea what I wanted to do with my life (a fact that must have worried my father-in-law). I was working as a laborer in an auto parts warehouse, stocking shelves and pulling parts. We used to have contests to see how big an engine block we could deadlift without help. Clearly, that was never going to be a career—but what else to do? I thought about studying law. Then somebody tried to convince me to sell insurance. Somebody else tried to get me to go to chiropractic school. None of that seemed right.

I had thought about vocational ministry, but truthfully I found it too intimidating. My father had become a pastor when I was a teenager, so I had some idea of what the job involved. I wasn't opposed to the idea, but pastoral work included tasks for which I considered myself to be poorly suited. Those tasks scared me. Over a process of months, however, the Lord put me into situations that forced me to perform the very tasks that I found most frightening. I learned two lessons. The first was that the Lord is quite able to do His work through someone who is simply willing to be used—availability is more important than perceived ability. The second was that I actually enjoyed performing some of those dreaded tasks, while others were not nearly as bad as I had supposed them to be. Furthermore, I discovered a remarkable blessing in getting to see the results. I found that the more I did those jobs, the more I wanted to do them.

My bride was also watching those events unfold, and

she was seeing the same things. When I finally said aloud, "I think the Lord might be calling me into ministry," she responded, "I know!" In that moment, something clicked into place. I knew what God's direction was for my life, and I was eager to embrace it. I never had to surrender anything. God gave me the desires of my heart.

Please don't misunderstand: I am not suggesting that sadness and hardship are never God's will. The author of Hebrews speaks of faithful people who were denied shelter, food, and clothing, and who faced mocking, beating, imprisonment, torture, and death (Heb 11:35–40). When the will of God is hard and unpleasant, however, it usually arrives in ways that leave us no choice. Either God brings us directly into difficult conditions, or else He confronts us with choices that involve clear biblical precepts and principles. Under those circumstances God has already made His will known in Scripture.

I am talking about times when we really do have to make a choice and we don't know what it should be. We are seeking God's leading. Under those conditions, *one* of the things that we should consider is our own inclinations and desires. These may well be among the components that God uses to lead us while we follow Him.

QUESTIONS FOR THOUGHT AND DISCUSSION

- Are there times when God's will appears unpleasant to you? Why do you suppose it seems that way?

- Can you think of legitimate pursuits that you wish were God's will for you but that you don't believe are? What makes you think they are not?
- Why would people think that God's leading has to be unpleasant?

11
YOUR SENSE OF VOCATION

In the last chapter I said that our inclinations are one of the keys to God's leading. I suggested that God often prepares us to do His will by giving us a desire to do the kind of thing He wants us to do. Indeed, I believe that this is one of the most important principles in finding God's direction—but it is also one of the most easily misunderstood. To avoid some of the misunderstandings, I'd like to take another chapter to clarify the notion of calling or vocation.

By the words *vocation* and *calling* I mean something like *station in life*. Every person occupies several stations in life: she or he holds a variety of callings. Being married is a calling, and so is being single. Parenthood is a calling. Your age, sex, ethnicity, and social standing are part of your calling. We often speak of a "call to ministry," but for Christians every station in life is a calling that is honorable and is a means to bring glory to God (1 Cor 7:17–23). Really, every kind of vocation and even avocation can and should be used as a ministry.

Fishing or quilting, for example, can provide opportunities to build relationships that open the door to share the gospel or to address other spiritual needs. Right now, however, I am concerned specifically with that aspect of vocation or calling that we often refer to as a *career* or a *life's work*. How should we decide upon a life's work?

Years ago I was riding a subway in Budapest. As I exited the train, I saw an underground kiosk selling some delicious-looking cream horns. Since I hadn't eaten in hours, I decided to treat myself to one. The Hungarian language is a mystery to me, so I pointed at the case. The vendor wrapped the pastry and we exchanged money. As I climbed the steps to street level, I opened the wrapper and took a big bite. I was expecting the kind of sugary, whipped-cream confection familiar to Americans. Instead, I got a mouthful of some rather sour-tasting white cheese. The contrast between what I expected and what I tasted was so great that I almost spat out the pastry. I threw the uneaten bit away.

Sometimes, we believe that we will enjoy something because of what we expect from it. It looks appealing. When we actually try the thing, however, it fails to live up to our expectations. We are disappointed because what we thought we liked was an imagined idea of the thing, not the thing itself.

While our inclinations are an important key to discerning God's leading, we must evaluate them rightly. We must incline toward the thing *as it is* rather than toward the thing *as we imagine it to be*. We can be drawn to vocations for wrong reasons as easily as I was drawn toward that pastry for the wrong reason. When that happens and when the things do not live up to our expectations, we are inevitably disappointed.

I know of a very good musician who earned a doctorate, but who hated teaching music once he found a job. He eventually got a law degree and switched careers. I also know of a lawyer who simply doesn't enjoy working with the law; she is good, but her job is drudgery for her. I know of a woman who felt drawn to nursing because she thought she wanted to help people. To her dismay, she found that she didn't like to be around the sick, and she soon left nursing for a different career. In vocations as in cream horns, we don't always actually enjoy what we think we should enjoy.

Even worse, people sometimes choose a vocation not for itself but for the benefits that they believe it will confer. They don't really find the work appealing, but they want the money, the social standing, the reputation, or the power that comes with the job. A job that appeals to your *pride*, however, is not necessarily the same as a job that will appeal to *you*. Choosing a calling for its perceived benefits may well lead to misery.

How can you tell whether your inclination is genuine and whether a particular vocation is yours? A full answer to that question could take a whole book by itself. Here, I can only offer the following considerations to guide you. Before you settle on a career, you should ask yourself these questions seriously.

First, have you learned to work? Every worthwhile calling takes hard work. Every job comes with moments of drudgery and with unpleasant tasks that you just have to muscle through. You are not in a position to consider a calling until you have learned to show up on time, respect structured authority, get along with your co-workers, avoid workplace intrigues, meet deadlines, and do an hour's labor for an hour's pay. Master these skills first; worry about a vocation later.

Second, what kind of work do you most like to do? Too many people begin by asking what kind of job they would like to have, but having a job and doing the work are two different things. What kind of work are you passionate about? What would you do as a hobby, even if nobody ever recognized it or paid you to do it? Do you enjoy manual tasks? Intellectual activity? Solving problems? Helping people? Building things? Creating art? Learning what kind of work you most enjoy will help to steer you away from false impressions about the kind of job you only think you'd like. Your enjoyment and your calling should go together.

Third, what kind of work are you gifted for? What do you do well? Different people excel at different things. Let me use my extended family as an example. My brother has great engineering skills. From the time he was a child he was putting up towers and building radios. He ended up as a chief engineer reporting to the governor of a Midwestern state. One of my sisters is skilled as a helper of people. She oozes compassion and care, so it's not surprising that she has become a nurse. My father excels at developing relationships (he never met a stranger) and coordinating people. He was a successful, upwardly-mobile manager in an airline until he left that calling to become a pastor. And me? For more than two decades my life has revolved around students, books, classrooms, teaching schedules, and grading (which I admit that I have to muscle through). It's amazing how one family can include people with such diverse interests and skills—and I haven't even told you about my wife, my mother, my other siblings, or my children.

You need to pay attention both to what you enjoy doing and to what you do well. One way to accomplish that is to try lots of different tasks. That's one reason why high schools and colleges require a varied curriculum supplemented by multiple extracurricular activities. You are given the opportunity to test yourself in several directions. If you do some volunteering (such as in your local church), you can test yourself in even more. Don't be afraid to try a task just because it is new. You may discover a new love.

Fourth, what kind of work is needed? Is a particular kind of work worth doing? Not every activity contributes equally to human wellbeing, even if you enjoy it and are good at it. Furthermore, even if the work is worth doing, are too many people already trying to do it? For example, you might like to collect trading cards. You may be a very competent card collector. Nevertheless, collecting and dealing in trading cards can only provide a living for a limited number of people. To some extent, the same principle applies to other callings. The world needs only a finite number of oncologists, constitutional lawyers, heavy equipment operators, stockbrokers, or disc jockeys. Callings tend to run through cycles when they are either more or less at capacity. Before you choose any calling, you might ask how useful the calling is and whether any more people are really needed to fulfill it.

Fifth, what kind of work are you qualified for? Every job above minimum wage requires you to meet some kind of qualifications. A vocation is not something that is handed to you. It is something that you earn. You can't write software if you don't know code. You can't be a pilot if you don't learn to fly. You can't be a rancher if you can't handle stock. You can't be a farmer if you can't plow a furrow. You can't be a tailor if you don't know how to sew. One of the differences between a vocation and an avocation is that you must measure up to the qualifications.

Finally, what kind of work have you been confirmed into? Most vocations require some sort of outside recognition or accreditation. Plumbers, electricians, boilermakers, and machinists have to pass examinations to be certified. Ministers are examined by councils and then ordained. Lawyers have to pass a bar exam. Even where your vocation does not involve formal certification, your peers within that vocation can offer their evaluation and confirmation of your suitability for their field.

One more thing. Most vocations are not set in stone. Like my friend who tried music but went into law, and like my father who supervised employees in an airline but became a pastor, you may find a new vocation that fits you better. Even within the same general vocation you may find that you end up doing more than one thing. In my case, I taught in a college for two years after I graduated from seminary. Then I spent around fifteen years in pastoral ministry. Over twenty years ago I arrived at the seminary where I presently teach theology, and during my time here I've gone back and forth between teaching and administration. With all those changes, I've never believed that I was leaving the will of God.

Choosing a vocation is not the decision of a moment. It involves a process of trying new activities, learning new skills, working hard to improve those skills, and judging both your inclinations and your suitability for those things. Under normal circumstances, you should not expect God to show in advance what you are going to do with the rest of your life. You should expect to discover your vocation over a process of time and effort, and you should not be afraid to try more than one direction.

QUESTIONS FOR THOUGHT AND DISCUSSION

- Have you ever tried your hand at a task that you thought you'd enjoy, only to discover that it was not nearly as enjoyable as you'd imagined it would be? What was it, and why didn't you enjoy it?
- Have you ever had to engage in a task that you perceived as off-putting but discovered that you actually enjoyed it? What was it, and what did you enjoy about it?
- What jobs do you genuinely enjoy that contain elements you find tedious or repellant? How do you get yourself through the less enjoyable parts of the job?

12

THE PEACE OF GOD

If God has an individual direction for His children, then they ought to be able to discern what that direction is. Yet how do we find God's leading without demanding some form of continuing, special revelation? How can we claim that we respect the sufficiency and finality of Scripture if God can somehow lead us while we are making decisions?

Many Christians believe that the way to find God's will is to pay attention to a kind of subjective inner sense. Through this feeling or intuition God somehow communicates that He wants us to make one decision and not another. People who claim to experience this inner sense speak of it as a feeling of peace. For evidence that God provides this inner peace they appeal to Colossians 3:15, which commands believers to let the peace of God (or peace of Christ) rule in our hearts. The word *rule* is a term that means to *umpire* or *decide*. Consequently, these people conclude that God leads them through the sense of peace that He gives them.

Others have objected that leading through such an inner sense would be equivalent to extra-Scriptural revelation. Many even reject the notion that God causes subjective impressions at all. They insist that believers must rely solely upon the written Word of God rather than upon inner impressions.

I see merit in that response. I agree that the written Scriptures must be the Christian's only source of spiritual authority. On the other hand, I think that this objection can be overstated and misapplied—and I am not alone. Most Christians in most places at most periods of church history have acknowledged that God can indeed cause subjective impressions that do not involve new revelation. I am willing to entertain the possibility that God can produce some sort of non-revelatory intuition in the conscience of the believer.

We have plenty of evidence that God does work subjectively within people. For one thing, the Spirit of God produces conviction of sin—and we have all felt it at some point (John 16:7–11). For another, God's Spirit also gives us an inner witness that leads us to welcome the Bible as God's Word (1 Cor 2:12–16). Furthermore, the Spirit Himself bears witness with our spirit that we are the children of God (Rom 8:15–16). All of these are points at which God creates subjective impressions within people, but these impressions are not new revelations outside of the Bible.

Many believe that this kind of impression is in view in Colossians 3:15. They believe that the command, "let the peace of God rule in your hearts," shows how God leads us through an inner sensation. I disagree. My reason for rejecting this interpretation is that Paul immediately adds, "to which [peace] also ye are called in one body." In other words, the peace that Paul writes about to the Colossians is not an inner sensation. It is an outward manner of relating to other believers in the church. This peace of God is to govern our hearts *as we carry out our Christian relationships*. While I believe that some intuitions or subjective impressions can come from God, I would not appeal to this verse to prove the point.

Indeed, believers who make this subjective, inner sense the chief or only way of discerning God's direction are asking for trouble. Even if God *can* prompt inner sensations, He does not *promise* that He will guide us with those impressions. To rely upon something that God has not promised is simply presumptuous. It is a form of tempting God.

As I've already said, I believe that God is able to prompt certain kinds of sensations or subjective feelings within the believer. Some of these subjective feelings are listed as fruit of the Spirit (Gal 5:22–23), i.e., love, joy, and peace. Yet nothing in the text indicates that inner sensations are produced *only* by God's Spirit. We know as a matter of experience that subjective impressions come from sources other than God. Our inner sensations are affected by how tired or hungry we are, by what we eat, and by whatever stresses we may be experiencing. We have no clear way of saying with certainty whether a particular sense of inner peace (or any other sense of leading) is coming from God or from too much cabbage.

Why, then, do I continue to grant subjective impressions a role in seeking God's leading? Further, how do I avoid seeing these sensations as new revelations from God? Let me explain.

I'll tackle the second question first, and its answer will lead us back to the first question. I don't believe that inner impressions have to constitute new revelations because God can act upon the conscience in the same ways that He acts upon the rest of the created order: either directly or indirectly. If God acts directly and immediately upon the created order, then we call it a *miracle*. If He acts indirectly through secondary causes, we call it *Providence*.

Since God can providentially produce effects within nature, I see no reason to deny that He can produce subjective impressions within the conscience in the same way. Indeed, God clearly does use secondary causes to prompt our consciences: one example is the conviction that we feel when we are rebuked for our sins. This conviction is not miraculous or revelatory, but providential. God can also move our consciences and shape our feelings through other secondary causes, some of which we have already discussed: Scripture, duties, counsel, circumstances, and so forth.

From the divine side, God can operate within our hearts and minds while not manipulating them directly. From the human side, much can be explained by the marvelous ways in which our minds work. The human mind is able to sift, combine, and evaluate complicated sets of factors very rapidly at a level beneath conscious deliberation. That's why we can sometimes fall asleep pondering a question and then wake up knowing the answer. It's also why we can sometimes intuit conclusions without really being aware of how we reach them.

These intuitions often give us a sense of the right answer.

Working providentially, God can use these mental powers to prompt a sense of His leading within His people. This sense is not miraculous. It does not demand the direct action of God upon the soul. It is not revelatory. Instead, God leads providentially by prompting inner direction through secondary agencies.

Given these considerations, I do not believe that we should simply ignore all inner impressions when we are looking for God's leading. All the same, I must speak a word of caution. Since this leading is providential, it involves an element of human interpretation. Consequently, our inner sense of leading or peace must never be taken as infallible. As with other factors, our subjective sense of God's leading needs to be evaluated, weighed, and considered. We must not treat it as if it were a form of divine revelation.

The fact that this sense is not revelation also implies that we should not look to it as the primary key to God's leading. We should take inner impressions into account, but they should hardly ever be the determining factor when we are seeking God's direction. An inner sense of peace can help to assure us that we are on the right track, but it does not take the place of the other factors. We ought to use these inner, subjective impressions to verify decisions that we are making primarily by weighing the other considerations. In other words, we should use the inner sense of peace for confirmation, not information.

One more thing. We are not all equally intuitive. We are not equally reflective. We are not equally aware of our feelings and inner states. We have not all enjoyed (or endured) the same experiences, and intuition tends to be sharpened by the variety of experiences. If you are a less intuitive person, then you may not feel a sense of leading or peace about a given decision. In fact, you may never experience such a sense. If you don't, that's fine. God is still able to lead you. Please don't insist, however, that the inner experience of others means nothing.

On the other hand, if you are a more intuitive person, you may need to be careful of overestimating your inner sense of peace and direction. You will need to compare it to the other criteria that we have discussed. Furthermore, you shouldn't look down upon people who never experience the same inner sensations that you do.

What I am trying to do is to stake out a middle ground on this issue. I think that it is wrong to ignore our subjective impressions about God's leading. For one thing, those feelings may come providentially from God. For another, they may simply be good intuitions. Nevertheless, we must not respond to those feelings as if they were a sure revelation of God's will, especially since they can also come from other sources. If we avoid both extremes, we can legitimately consider our subjective feelings, inner impressions, or intuitions as one factor among several when we are seeking God's leading. Nevertheless, we should take account of these subjective impressions only after we have carefully weighed all the other considerations.

QUESTIONS FOR THOUGHT AND DISCUSSION

- Have you ever experienced an inner sense of what was a right decision or what you ought to do in a particular situation? Do you believe that God can lead you that way?
- What would you say to a person who claimed an inner "leading" about what another person should do (for example, "I sense that God wants you to marry that man," or, "I have peace that God's will is for you to invest in that stock")?
- Is there any difference between saying, "I have peace about this decision," and saying, "God told me to do this"? If so, what is the difference?

13
BUYER'S BLUES

Years ago I began an unsuccessful career in sales. When I started, my manager warned me that I would have to learn to help people get past what he called "Buyer's Blues." What is Buyer's Blues? As my manager explained it, many people experience feelings of doubt, anxiety, panic, and guilt either immediately before or immediately after the decision to make a significant purchase. Part of my job as a salesman would be to coax people through their Buyer's Blues so they would finalize the sale.

Since then I've noticed the same phenomenon in the lives of Christians who face big decisions. Sometimes they are so afraid of missing God's will that they cannot bring themselves to make a choice. Other times they make the choice, but then they immediately regret the decision they've made.

Buyer's Blues can be exacerbated by circumstances. One of my friends accepted a pastorate in Alaska. Driving up the ALCAN Highway, his moving van blew a tire. The rental company took days to send help. Then the "help" overturned his moving van, spilling his possessions along the highway and damaging many of his goods. This was only one episode in a nightmare move. Finally, another friend told him, "It's obvious that you've missed God's will."

My friend didn't listen to that counsel, but others might. I've seen Christians who gauge their grasp of God's leading by how well the decision works. If the going gets tough, they assume that they must have missed the will of God. If they have smooth sailing, then they assume that God approves their decision.

When things don't seem to work out well, does that mean we've blown it and landed ourselves outside God's will? And if we have missed His will, is there any way back, or are we doomed to some permanent spiritual disability? I suggest the following by way of answer.

First, we are not always able to gauge what is working since we don't always know what God is doing. What seems to work in the short run may be very different from what actually works in the long run. People who are clearly following God's will can sometimes experience very unpleasant consequences in the immediate aftermath of their decisions. For example, Paul and Silas were beaten and thrown into prison (Acts 16:16–24). The book of Hebrews speaks of faithful believers who were cruelly mocked, whipped, chained, imprisoned, stoned, and killed, who had inadequate clothing and money, who endured suffering and even torment, and who were even left without a home. The text adds that the world was not worthy of them (Heb 11:36–38). Their decisions to follow God's will resulted in extreme hardships, but God placed His approval upon them.

Along that same line, my friend who made that nightmare of a move to Alaska ended up spending decades pastoring there. He enjoyed a fruitful ministry. In fact, he retired from that church. The difficulties of the move were no indication of God's displeasure.

Second, God's leading is neither miraculous nor prophetic. God leads through Providence, and because His leading is providential, it does not yield certainty. Therefore, as long as we are following the precepts and principles of Scripture, God's leading is not a simple matter of obedience or disobedience. It is more akin to the exercise of wisdom and sound judgment. It is possible for us to make an apparently-sound decision that turns out to be a mistake, at least from some points of view.

Third, God is quite capable of using our mistakes. In fact, since judgment and wisdom grow as we make decisions, and since making decisions involves making mistakes, God must intend that we make at least some mistakes. We learn to make good decisions through experience. We gain experience by making bad decisions. While we cannot blame our mistakes on God, we can trust Him to help us make the best of them.

Fourth, growth in character relies upon endurance, and endurance requires suffering (Rom 5:3–4). Whether we are in the will of God or not, some of our choices will result in unexpectedly difficult circumstances. The order in which God produces spiritual maturity is (1) suffering, (2) endurance, (3) character, (4) hope. His will is for His children to suffer enough to require them to show endurance, which will build up their character, eventually producing hope or anticipation. We cannot always judge whether our choice was according to God's leading by whether it leads to a rose-strewn future.

Fifth, every choice, whether mistaken or not, opens a new path in front of us. Once we are on that path, there is no point asking how we might have fared had we chosen a different path. God's will is always that we tread our present path in the best way that we can to bring glory to Him. Part of going forward includes "forgetting those things which are behind" (Phil 3:13). We have no true knowledge of what might have been. We never really know how things might have turned out had we chosen otherwise. Habitual second-guessing of our choices only makes us miserable now.

Sixth, our new choices often bring with them new obligations. These obligations will determine at least some part of God's will for the future. For example, the time to ask whether God is leading you to marry a particular person is *before* the nuptials. During the wedding you swear oaths that are lifelong and binding. God never wills that you violate your wedding vows. Once you are married, you must never think that God's will was for you to marry someone else. God's will is for you to remain committed to your marriage and for that marriage to succeed.

Similarly, if you have run up debt on your credit cards, God's will is that you pay what you owe. You may decide that the charges were unwise and out of God's will (and they may have been), but that no longer matters. God's will is for you to fulfill your obligations, even if doing so means *not* doing some other things that you might once have thought were God's leading.

Seventh, sometimes we make choices that we later discover to be conspicuously bad. If nothing binds us to those choices, then we might be able to retrace our steps. Bad choices come from not paying attention to the criteria for good choices—criteria such as those that we have discussed in previous chapters. Bad choices may not always be sinful, but they are choices for which we are obviously unsuited. When that happens, we should recognize the difference between endurance (which is a virtue) and obstinance in folly (which is a form of vicious pride). When we *can* correct a bad choice, then we *should* correct it.

Eighth, we must learn to be perplexed without despairing (2 Cor 4:8). We have no guarantee that we'll be able to make every choice with confidence. We have no assurance that every choice will work out well. After all, even with access to direct, divine revelation, the apostle Paul made choices that landed him in horrible circumstances. Some Bible teachers still question whether each of those choices really represented God's will for Paul's life. One even wrote a book entitled *Blunders of Paul*.

What distinguished Paul was not necessarily that he made the right choice every time (though I disagree with the assertion that his ministry was filled with blunders). What distinguished him was that, even in the worst of circumstances, he kept pressing forward in the ways that matter most: seeking to minister the gospel, strengthen the saints, and glorify Christ. Indeed, the entire epistle to the Philippians is a testimony to this aspect of his life.

As far as I know, the Bible contains no promise that God will give us absolute certainty in our important choices. My personal testimony is that I have rarely experienced that degree of confidence. Often I have had to make major decisions without even ninety or eighty percent probability. Sometimes I have made them with only the slightest inclination in one direction: fifty-one percent or less. I have made decisions that were followed by joyful excitement; I have also made decisions that were followed by shattering experiences with Buyer's Blues. That doesn't mean that those choices were out of God's will or that I didn't have His leading.

God doesn't seem to be interested in having us torture ourselves with regret. He doesn't want us constantly to be looking over our shoulder, wondering whether each choice that we made was "in His will." Yes, God does have a plan for each individual believer, and He does lead His children. If we are seeking to honor Him, if we are choosing within the bounds of Scripture, and if we are employing the canons of wisdom and careful choosing, then we can trust Him to guide us providentially into the choices that He wants us to make. We can choose carefully. We should choose boldly.

QUESTIONS FOR THOUGHT AND DISCUSSION

- Have you ever made a choice that seemed to

turn out badly in the short run but eventually proved to be the right choice?
- Have you ever made a decision that you thought was good at the time but that you later became convinced was wrong? Were you able to retrace your steps and change the decision?
- Can you think of examples where the Bible commends people for making decisions that went badly for them in the short run?

AFTERWORD: SO YOU'VE MADE A BAD DECISION

Every pastor can tell stories about Christians who make bad decisions. Sometimes their decisions are not merely bad, but sinful. Any Christian can make decisions that are entirely outside God's will.

Of course, God does not let His children go on sinning. He brings conviction and chastening into their lives. God authorizes churches to call their members into account and even to disfellowship them over some sins. Genuine believers who sin will eventually reach a point at which they realize that their sin is exacting a terrible cost. They will understand that they are out of God's will, and they wish that they were back in it. The question is whether, having once abandoned God's will, anyone can find a way back again. One of the worst parts about being out of God's will is that the way back seems so doubtful.

A similar doubt can plague people who committed certain kinds of sins even before they were saved. Some sins produce greater long-term consequences than others, and some sins lead to greater regret than others. Even though their sins have been forgiven, some Christians can remain frozen by regret over sins that they once committed. They may doubt whether God fully accepts them or whether He provides any way forward for them.

Are you a Christian who is staggering under the burden of sinful choices? Then you need to know that Christ offers hope. He offers the hope of a way back to Himself. He offers hope of a way upward in the Christian life as you grow in grace and in your fellowship with Him. He offers the hope of a way forward into a life that is blessed and useful for Him.

Here are some examples of people who need hope.

Clarisse was a young woman when she found herself with an unwanted pregnancy. She chose to end her pregnancy with an abortion. In fact, she ended up having multiple abortions. Then she heard the gospel and was saved. She met a Christian man whom she married. As she studied the Bible, she came to understand that the embryos she had aborted were actually children. She was horrified by what she had done. She realized that she had made a very bad decision.

George was a Christian engineer climbing the corporate ladder. When he was asked to take over his company's office in a Middle-Eastern country, the adventure and responsibility appealed to him. So did the phenomenal salary and the substantial bonus. He accepted the job on the spot. When he told his wife, however, she was less than enthusiastic. She hated the thought of living halfway around the world from their families. She asked him where they could find Christian fellowship in a Muslim country. She also expressed concern because she and George wanted to have children, and the Middle East did not seem like a good place to raise a family. As she pointed out these facts, George realized that he had made a bad decision.

Abigail had been converted as a child and reared in a Bible-believing church. She had been warned from childhood that she should not date unsaved men, but no Christian men her age seemed to be available. Then she met Jake. He was not a Christian, but he was an upright and moral man. Abigail agreed to go out with him. Eventually the two of them fell in love. Although Abigail knew that it was wrong, she married Jake. Only then did she begin to understand how incompatible their perspectives were. She began to long for Christian fellowship and teaching, but Jake seemed to resent her efforts to restore her relationship with God.

All of these stories involve people who made sinful decisions: an abortion, a thoughtless promise, an unequal yoke. All of these people found that their bad choices brought consequences. Each of them came to understand that those choices were out of God's will. Each wishes to go forward in God's will. The question is, how do they get there?

In every case, the initial answer is the same. After a sinful choice, the way back begins with repentance. What does that mean? Repentance is essentially a change of perspective. Before repenting, sinners look at their sin as a worthwhile thing. They may know that it is wrong, but they judge the sin to be worth the consequences. Repentance means that they acknowledge how very wrong their sin is. They come to see it as God sees it, and they say the same thing about it that God says. Repentance means that if they faced the same choice again, they would want to reject the sin and obey the Lord.

The proper expression of repentance is to confess the sin (1 John 1:9). Confession involves two elements. The first element is to admit what we have done. God wants us to name the sin that we have committed. True confession is specific confession. When we confess our sins, we must offer no excuses and we must not try to shift the blame.

The second element of confession is to acknowledge our deed to be truly sinful. This element involves coming to see our sin as God sees it (though surely we will not see it in its full wickedness, as He does). It means talking about our sin in the same way that God talks about it.

Psalm 51 is an excellent example of the second element in confession. David's sin had already been named: Nathan the prophet had seen to that. Everybody knew that the king had committed adultery with Bathsheba and had engineered the murder of her husband, Uriah. For months, however, David had tried to evade responsibility. In Psalm 51 he finally faced God and acknowledged the blackness of his deeds. He accepted responsibility, he exhibited a broken spirit and a contrite heart, and he acknowledged that his sin had disrupted his fellowship with God. That is what true confession of sin looks like.

To whom should we confess our sins? Obviously, every sin is committed against God, so every sin must be confessed to Him. Often our sins also affect other people. A good rule of thumb is that we should confess our sins to anyone who is hurt by our sins. Sins committed only against God should be confessed to God. Sins that hurt another person should be confessed to that person. If the sin is a public matter, then public confession to the church may be necessary.

In the examples above, George needs to confess his sin to his wife as well as to God. Abigail needs to confess her sin to those godly counselors whose warnings she ignored by dating an unsaved man. Clarisse should acknowledge her past to her husband, and she would do well to make sure that her pastor knows about it as well.

The wonderful thing about confession is that it clears the air spiritually. God is faithful and just to forgive every confessed sin, which means that those sins no longer block our fellowship with Him. Confession is also a mechanism through which we receive cleansing from sins. In other words, God removes the pollution from our souls. Just as importantly, confession is a major step in restoring our relationship with others against whom we have sinned. When we confess the wrongs that we have done against others, then they have the opportunity to extend forgiveness to us in ways that we can realize.

Repentant confession paves the road back to God. When we know that we have sinned, we need to change our mind about the sin and to acknowledge our wrongdoing. When we have made choices that have violated God's will, then God's will is that we repent and confess. If we are willing to take this step in God's will, we will find that God welcomes us back to Him. Repentant Christians can always hope for a way back.

They can also hope for a way upward. God saves us to bring us into fellowship with Him. Although our familiar fellowship with God is damaged when we sin, confession restores that communion. Once we have confessed our sins, God's will for us is to go on growing in that fellowship, or, as Peter puts it, to grow in grace and in the knowledge of our Lord and Savior Jesus Christ (2 Pet 3:18). God wants every believer to progress from spiritual infancy to spiritual maturity (1 Cor 3:1–4; Heb 5:12–14). Progressive sanctification is God's will for every believer.

The fact is that nobody experiences unbroken growth in the Christian life. All believers sin sometimes, and until our sin is dealt with it impedes our spiritual growth (1 John 1:8–10). All of us sometimes need to confess our sins and to receive the promised forgiveness and cleansing. When we do that, we find that the impediment to fellowship and growth has been lifted. As those who have experienced God's great grace, we usually find ourselves motivated to redouble our activity toward spiritual growth. While God never wishes us to sin, He does find ways to use our past experience of sins to move us upward in the present. When we have sinned, Christ gives us hope of a way upward.

He also gives us hope of a way forward. The problem is that, as we seek to move forward, we will discover that sin still produces consequences. Some of those consequences will be temporary, but others may be permanent, depending upon the nature of the sins that we have committed. To move forward we must be prepared to accept the consequences of our sins.

For example, George made a commitment that he had no right to make. His rapid agreement to go to the Middle East was a betrayal of his previous commitment to love his wife (Eph 5:25–29). Consequently, God's will is for George to face his employers and ask to be released from a responsibility that he accepted too precipitously. Depending on his company, reneging on that agreement may affect George's future opportunities. He should embrace those consequences as lessons in making future choices more wisely.

God's will for Abigail is that she must not abandon her unsaved husband (1 Cor 7:12–16). Instead, she should become the best wife that she can be (1 Pet 3:1–6), submitting to her husband in every area that does not contradict Scripture. Her husband's interests may limit the degree to which she can be actively involved in her church, but by serving her husband she is also serving her Lord. Still, she should become as involved as he will permit, and she should continue her own growth in grace and knowledge.

The point is that the Lord always provides some path forward when we truly repent of our sins. We may not be able to do all that we would have done if we had not sinned, but we can still do something. God has a way to bless us and use us within His will.

Clarisse is a wonderful illustration of this principle. As she acknowledged her sin, and as she grew in her fellowship with Christ, she was asked to take the leadership of a crisis pregnancy center. In His grace, God began to use her past experience of sin as a way of opening new doors to ministry. Clarisse could understand the desperation that young women often feel when they have an unwanted pregnancy. She was able to help them in ways that would not occur to most other people.

The Lord is gracious and merciful. When our hearts have been broken over sin we may feel as if we will never be any good to Him, but He welcomes us back to Himself. He invites us into His fellowship and asks us to find pleasure in Him. He delights to take broken instruments and use them for His glory. Neither our future fellowship with God nor our future usefulness to Him have to be controlled by the sins of the past.

Saul of Tarsus was a mighty great sinner. He persecuted the church of Christ and engineered the stoning of Stephen. Even after he was saved he acknowledged that he was the chief of sinners (1 Tim 1:15). He might have wallowed in regret over his past sins. Instead, he took the attitude that, "forgetting those things which are behind, and reaching forth unto those things which are before, I press toward the mark for the prize of the high calling of God in Christ Jesus" (Phil 3:13–14). That is the attitude that God wants to see in every believer.

Sinful choices are always bad choices. They will always end up costing more than we want to pay. Nevertheless, God provides a way back, a way upward, and a way forward. The Bible is full of sinners whom God welcomed and used. So if you've sinned, God's will is that you repent and confess, that you grow in sanctification, and that, while you accept the consequences of your sin, you should live your life with confidence that He will bless you and use you.

APPENDIX A: WORKSHEET FOR DISCERNING GOD'S LEADING

State in clear words the decision that you are trying to make:

1. Does anything about this decision contradict what you know from Scripture?

2. Are you willing to do whatever God wants you to do? Is that apparent in the decisions you're already making?

3. Do you have any duties or obligations that should affect this decision?

4. Have you prayed carefully about this decision?

5. What do you need to know to make a wise decision? Have you informed yourself?

6. Have you sought counsel from your pastor, your spouse, your parents, or other godly people? What do your counselors say?

7. How do your circumstances affect this decision?

8. If the choice were simply up to you, what would you really like to do?

9. Do you have any inner sense that one decision is better or more pleasing to God than another?

10. Are you prepared to deal with the consequences if things get difficult after you make your decision?

APPENDIX B: IS THERE A CALL TO MINISTRY?

When my father was a new believer, he sensed a leading toward vocational Christian service. He sought the counsel of an older minister and told him, "I think the Lord is calling me into ministry."

The veteran pastor replied, "Forget it."

Surprised by this response, my father asked, "What do you mean, *forget it*?"

The old man answered, "Just what I said. Forget it. If you can forget it, then the Lord is not calling you into ministry. But if every time you bow your head to pray it's there, and if every time you open the Bible it convicts you, then you'd better pay attention."

My father tried to "forget it" for the next ten years —but he could not. Eventually he moved our family across the country to attend a Bible college, then accepted his first pastorate.

Christian people sometimes struggle to know whether God is calling them into ministry. Does the Bible teach that God calls individuals to be pastors? If so, then how can people know whether they have experienced that call? Furthermore, how do they know when God is leading them from one place of ministry to another?

As we have discussed in previous chapters, a calling is simply a station in life. Both celibacy and marriage are callings. Motherhood and fatherhood are callings. Youth and old age are callings. Christians have a calling to certain attitudes and patterns of life (1 Cor 7:15). A life's work (or *career*, to use the popular term) is a calling. In the New Testament, callings such as these are not distinguished from a calling to ministry. Indeed, all callings are to be used to bring glory and praise to God (1 Cor 7:17–40).

A call to vocational ministry is not qualitatively different from any of these. It differs primarily, and perhaps only, in the thing to which someone is being called. Therefore, virtually everything that I said in the chapter on vocation is also applicable here. In the interest of being more specific, however, I want to offer several considerations about a call to ministry.

Before I say anything else, though, I should mention one thing that is *not* a call to vocational ministry. We live in a world that is filled with spiritual need. Billions of lost people have never heard of Christ. Millions of professing Christians have misunderstood the gospel. Multitudes of believers have failed to apply the full teachings of God's Word to their lives, in some cases because no one has ever explained to them what the Bible actually says. People are desperate for spiritual leadership. Some people perceive these needs so acutely that they assume they are called to be pastors or

APPENDIX B: IS THERE A CALL TO MINISTRY?

missionaries. The perception of need, however, does not constitute a call.

On his second missionary journey Paul and his companions passed through Phrygia and Galatia, where the Holy Spirit specifically forbade them to preach in Asia (Acts 16:6). They tried to get into Mysia, but the Spirit would not allow them there either (Acts 16:7). They saw needs in both Asia and Mysia, but God did not call them to minister to those needs—at least, not at that time. The need did not constitute a call.

Spiritual needs exist everywhere. There will almost always be someplace where the needs seem more acute than they do in the place where you are laboring at the moment. As a rule, meeting any sort of need anywhere takes perseverance and sustained effort. If you are constantly drawn away from one labor to another because the needs seem greater, then you will never have the stability and consistency that are fundamental to meeting those needs. Do not be easily drawn away simply by a sense of the need. Just because you see the need does not mean that you are called to meet it.

What, then, might constitute a call? One of the most important passages for understanding this concept is 1 Timothy 3:1–5. In this text Paul is discussing the office of bishop or overseer, which I take to be the same office as both pastor and elder (Acts 20:17, 28; 1 Pet 5:1–4). The text mentions several elements that go into a call to ministry.

The first element is a desire for the office and work of a bishop. Paul uses two words that can be translated *desire*. The first means something like *aspire*, and the aspiration is to the office of overseer. The second word has the idea of a *longing* or *strong desire*; it is the same word that is sometimes translated *lust*. This strong desire is for the work.

Some men fall in love with the idea of being a minister. Perhaps they are drawn by the fact that pastors are on public display. Perhaps they are attracted by the respect that pastors receive. Perhaps they see the pastorate as an easy job with a light schedule (certainly a false impression) or a good way to make money (also usually false). These desires are all grounded in the wrong things, and people who are drawn to ministry for these reasons do not really aspire to the office. They do not long for the work. They are really attracted to a false image of what the ministry entails.

You cannot develop a right desire for ministry in the abstract. You will learn to aspire to the office and to long for the work as you begin to engage in the activities that pastors perform. You will be given opportunities to teach or preach the Scriptures. You will find yourself studying so that you will know what you are talking about. You will bump up against people with spiritual needs. You will begin to invest in those people and to give them a place in your life. As you grow in your knowledge of the Word, and as you develop the skill to influence people toward the gospel and all that follows it, you may find that you begin to love what you are doing. Out of that love, you may aspire to the office of overseer and long to do the kind of good work that an overseer does.

Desire is the first element in a call to the ministry. The second element is *qualification*. Indeed, the main thrust of 1 Timothy 3:1–5 is to list the qualifications for a bishop. Most of these are personal and moral qualifications that describe the pattern of a man's life. Incidentally, I say *a man* because the New Testament never lists any qualifications for female pastors, and it lists some that are not compatible with femininity. Maleness is one qualification for pastors, and men who want to be pastors must be irreproachable. Their lives must be characterized by restraint, prudence, respectability, hospitality, sobriety, stability, gentleness, diplomacy, generosity, and maturity. These qualifications speak more about the kind of man that a bishop is rather than the sort of tasks at which he is skilled.

Nevertheless, ministry does require certain gifts or skills, so the third element in a call to ministry is *giftedness*. Paul mentions two functional qualifications in 1 Timothy 3:1–5. The first is that a bishop must be an able teacher (1 Tim 3:2). The second is that he must be a good manager, as evidenced by his management of his own household (1 Tim 3:5). The first skill plays directly into his ability to feed Christ's sheep. The second supports his ability to care for the church of God.

A pastor must know the Scriptures well. Furthermore, he must be able to communicate and apply them clearly. This ability is not merely a native giftedness but a gift that has been improved through study, discipline, and practice. Consequently, as R. V. Clearwaters used to say, a call to minister is also a call to prepare.

These three elements—desire, qualifications, and giftedness—are mentioned explicitly in this one key text. To these three we can add at least one more element, which I will label *confirmation*. What I mean is this: in the New Testament, nobody ever declares himself to be a pastor on his own initiative. For that matter, nobody gets unilaterally appointed to the pastorate by some other individual. The New Testament never depicts anyone becoming a pastor without being recognized as one by the church that he serves. In other words, in the New Testament, the call to ministry is a call *by a church*.

A man may desire the office of a bishop and he may long for the work. He may meet all of the personal qualifications that Scripture spells out. He may be marvelously gifted. He may have improved his gifts in remarkable ways. Even so, he is not called to be a pastor until a church calls him. The call from the congregation confirms what the man desired and what others may have thought. The Lord does not call anyone except by the approval of a church.

A man becomes a pastor when he is called by a congregation and he accepts the call. The church will typically license him as a minister. Eventually the church may call for a council of pastors and messengers from churches of like faith and order. These pastors and messengers will examine the minister for his Christian experience, qualifications, gifts, and doctrine. If they are satisfied with his call, then they will recommend that the church ordain him to the gospel ministry. Ordination does not make him a pastor, but it does provide an additional layer of public confirmation for his calling.

Of course, Christians also recognize other functions as vocational ministries besides pastor-bishop-elder. I'll give two examples. First, churches commission and support missionaries, most often through sending agencies. Second, Bible colleges and seminaries install professors who are usually ministers themselves to train future pastors. Furthermore, the administrators of these missions and schools, and of other ministries like Christian camps and publishing houses, are also ministers.

When we look at people like professors and agency presidents, we need to remember that pastors hold the only New Testament office of spiritual leadership. All parachurch organizations—sending agencies, seminaries, publishing houses, broadcasting ministries, camps, and so forth—are simply service organizations whose reason for being is to assist local churches in their ministries. Consequently, while we may view missionaries, professors, and agency presidents as vocational ministers, they are not pastors unless they also pastor a local church.

These other ministries require some of the same skills that a pastor must possess, but they also require some different skills. While people who fill these ministries should have the same kind of desire and character qualifications as a pastor, they may have to meet rather different functional qualifications. Furthermore, they will not be called to their positions by a church but by the agency that hires them. Generally, however, men who have been called to be pastors can move rather easily into one of these other positions, and vice versa.

How should one decide when the time has come to change ministries? This question is not different in kind from any other important decision that a person could be asked to make. The same principles apply to leaving a church for another ministry that would apply to making any change in employment, to getting married, or to deciding where to live. The only difference is that a ministry is more than a job. It involves a serious commitment that should not be dissolved for light reasons. Again, the same principles that govern all sober decision-making should govern these decisions as well.

There is such a thing as a call to ministry. At minimum, it is experienced through desire, qualifications, giftedness, and confirmation. Since few pastors remain in the same ministry for their entire lives, those who have experienced this call to ministry must also look for some element of leading between ministries. In doing so, they should appropriate the normal principles for discerning God's leading while making wise choices.